LEARN HOW TO MEDITATE

A Beginner's Step-by-Step
Guide and 90 Day Journal

This Guide Belongs to:

....

**PEACELAND
HAVEN**
Publications

www.peacelandhaven.com

Learn How to Meditate: A Beginner's Step-by-Step Guide and 90 Day Journal by Natalie Brown

PEACELAND HAVEN Publications

Sign up to our mailing list to get notified when we release new guides and journals.
https://bit.ly/aznbooksplh

Or scan the QR code below to subscribe.

TABLE OF CONTENTS

PART ONE

THE GUIDE

PART TWO

THE JOURNAL

PART ONE
THE GUIDE

INTRODUCTION

Welcome to your pathway to clarity and calm!

Did you know that meditation practice can help you refresh your mind and body, gain clarity, reduce anxiety, calm your thoughts, ease depression and help you become more focused and at peace with yourself and the world? The great thing is, you can do a meditation practice in as little as 1 minute!

There are many approaches, benefits, techniques, and schools of practice in meditation. You have purchased this guide and journal because you're looking for a simple overview and tips on getting started. In this beginner's guide, you'll learn fundamental principles to begin reaping the benefits of this ancient practice that will lead to clarity and peace in your life. What I am outlining for you aims to take the confusion out of the "how and why" and provide basic, easy-to-understand, practical information, actionable steps, instruction, and a journaling tool to get you started. This non–religious approach to meditation guides you in a simple, modern, and accessible way.

I decided to create this how-to guide to meditation with a journal because I wished I had access to something like this when I first started. I struggled to get simple, straightforward information, how-to steps on meditation practice, and direction to realistically incorporate it into my daily routine. Upon speaking with friends and other people interested in starting a meditation practice, I realized that a how-to guide and journal might help others more easily begin a regular practice, so I decided to write this guide with a journal combination.

Let me be clear and say that this is by no means an extensive book on meditation, all the history, spirituality, science, and the many types of practices that exist. This guide is a beginner's how-to that will get you started on your journey. I have compiled all the essential information I know from my 20 years of learning and practice to save you countless hours reading multiple books and articles and chasing down the rabbit hole. There is so much to mediation, and there are more advanced books and teachings available should you want to dive into the history or a specific technique or practice.

When I started meditation practice, I struggled incredibly with it for about two years. I was plagued by overwhelming, racing thoughts and many distractions, and I struggled to focus. I read many books on meditation and took classes, often feeling like there was something "wrong" with me or that meditation would just not work. I was so frustrated! I really struggled, and I think many people new to meditation have a similar experience, so they never truly get started or can keep up a consistent practice. I also feel that myths about meditation can scare a beginner off. I will cover the biggest myth in this guide.

Instead of giving up, I figured something was better than nothing. I started with 30 seconds of deep, focused breathing and gradually increased my time by 30 seconds. In the beginning, I focused on breathing only. I began to incorporate music with breathing and eventually learned about the different types of meditation. For me, the most enjoyable meditations are mantra/affirmation meditations and guided ones because I feel supported and encouraged. I can now sit for 45 minutes or longer if I desire to. I genuinely relish this time to go inside and be still, calm, and feel oneness with universal energy.

Not only has meditation helped me navigate debilitating critical thoughts, anxiety, personal loss, grief, depression, and PTSD (post traumatic stress disorder), it has helped me reconnect to my true essence, helped me connect to spirit, allowed me to experience clarity and peace, calmness, and a sense of well-being and purpose. Meditation has changed my life, but the change didn't happen in the blink of an eye. It has taken time, practice, and consistency.

Now I feel called to teach others to receive the gift of meditation. In the last few years, I have studied and certified to be able to guide and teach others. I love teaching and using meditation as one of the practices I use to help guide others working through changes in their lives. My heart desires to help you experience the immense benefits of this incredible daily practice.

As you begin, be kind to yourself and know that just showing up to your practice is a HUGE deal! Be gentle with yourself and know that you're doing fantastic. If you struggle, simply start observing your breath for 30 seconds knowing that's okay. Everyone's going to progress in their own time and in their way.

Meditation is the process of training your mind and spirit, and that can take time. Know that you are doing it perfectly by committing to this work daily and consistently. I'll help you understand that meditation is as natural as breathing and that anyone can (and should) do it!

In this guide, we will cover the following topics:
1. What Is Meditation?
2. Key Terms Used in Meditation Practice
3. The Biggest Myth About Meditation
4. The Objective of Meditation
5. Spirituality and Meditation
6. Why You Should Meditate
7. Benefits of Meditation
8. How Long You Should Meditate
9. 10 Steps To Start A Meditation Practice You Can Stick To
10. How to a Set Meditation Intention with Examples

WHAT IS MEDITATION?

For some beginners, meditation can seem quite intimidating. You might think you will never be able to rid yourself of overwhelming thoughts to do the practice. You might feel it's too time intensive. You might even think you could never sit still without fidgeting for a long time!

Meditation is an exercise for the brain and the spirit. The idea that your brain and body should stop working while you meditate is simply wrong. The essence of meditation is to create a "space" between you and what is your body and mind and allow space for connection to your spirit.

Meditation practice allows you to become the observer of your thoughts and what is going on in your body and spirit. The practice aims to train you to be in a state of peace and presence no matter what's happening inside your mind. An important aspect for some people is to unlock happiness and inspiration from deep inside. Meditation trains your mind to be unreceptive to distractions. Doing this gives your mind's natural inventiveness more space to reveal itself – and the conscious mind the means to take note of it.

So What *Exactly* is Meditation?

Simply put, meditation is a 2,500+ year-old practice for training the mind and tuning in to your spirit. When you take time to meditate, you allow yourself to become present, relaxed, and alert.

Most often, you focus your attention on one thing. Traditionally, the focus is your breath, a mantra or affirmation, which is a word or phrase you repeat during your meditation.

Meditation is an exercise that allows you to discover oneness and truth within yourself and helps you understand your energy. The brain and the body will benefit from this exercise, but this is only a side effect of a much more significant action. As you get into a regular practice, you'll enter into a highly relaxed and focused state of mind, which will often help you achieve incredible well-being, peace, and focus.

KEY TERMS USED IN MEDITATION PRACTICE

The words and phrases that follow are only a starting point. There are many different terms based on the style of meditation you practice. The following section provides some of the most commonly used words and phrases you will hear when you begin your meditation practice. *NOTE: some pronunciations will vary by dialect and region.*

Affirmation. The act of confirming something to be true or a written or oral statement that confirms something is true.

Allowing Stillness. This comes to you through the skill of using abandonment of effort within your body to enter abandonment of participation within your mind by "allowing" the mind to return to stillness.

Anapanasati. A Pali word (pronounced aanaa-paana-sati) that refers to the mindfulness of breathing.

Asana. The pose in which you sit in formal meditation (pronounced aa-suh-nuh). It should be comfortable and stable but also support alertness. Examples: Full or half Lotus, kneeling (Zen), or sitting in a straight-backed chair.

Back to Center or Centering. "Center" meaning the stillness and contentment of your inner Being. Centering allows you a moment of self-reflection. Centering also helps you be more in tune and aware of your feelings and overall mind-body well-being.

Beginner's Mind. A mind that is open to the moment's experience.

Chakra. The energy system (pronounced chaa-kruh). A Sanskrit word that translates literally to "disc" or "wheel." In yoga, meditation, and Ayurveda, chakra refers to psychoenergetic centers of the subtle body, also considered wheels of energy. The basic system has seven chakras: root, sacrum, solar plexus, heart, throat, third eye, and crown. Each chakra is associated with a color, element, syllable, significance, etc.

Come Back To Your Breath. Returning to regular–paced breathing during a meditation session. Often used when thoughts crowd the mind to get back in touch with yourself and be present.

Compassion. When you empathize with someone who is suffering and feel compelled to reduce the suffering. Compassion literally means "to suffer together."

Contemplation. A thoughtful, calm way of thinking of an idea.

Deep Sigh. This is the natural way to release tension in your body and brain and reset your nervous system. Breathe in deeply, then breathe out fully and for longer on the exhale.

Easy Pose (Sukhasana). It is the name for any comfortable, cross-legged, seated position and one of the most basic poses used in meditation and yoga practice. In this case, however, "easy" doesn't mean the opposite of difficult. It means "with ease." Sitting in Sukhasana (pronounced sue-car-sana) is sitting with ease in any way you can. For some people, using pillows, blankets, towels, and yoga blocks can help you feel as comfortable as possible in this pose.

Hand on the Heart. Used for a sense of grounding and safety in the moment. Placing your hand over your heart and breathing gently can soothe your mind and body. This practice takes advantage of breath, touch, and memories of feeling safe with another person.

Heaviness. The experience that arises within your body when it fully relaxes and your muscles no longer hold your weight.

Japa. A Sanskrit term (pronounced jaa-pa), also known as jaap, refers to the recitation or repetition of a word or phrase (mantra).

Kundalini. From the Hindu tradition (pronounced kuun-Da-li-nii). The "coiled" energy that is believed to reside at the base of your spine. A goal of meditation is to release or awaken this energy.

Lotus Position. The famous cross-legged position seen in almost all Hindu meditative practices.

Mala. A strand of 108 beads used in specific meditation techniques, similar to a Catholic rosary (pronounced MAH-lah).

Mantra. A word or sound is repeated to focus in meditation (pronounced MAAN-truh). Mantras can be a spiritual word, sound, syllable, or phrase that has a transformational effect on the mind. You can repeat mantras silently or out loud. Repeating a mantra helps the mind go beyond thought to move into the silence to profound levels of awareness.

Meditation Instructor or Meditation Guide. A person authorized and trained to give meditation instruction.

Meta–awareness (meta consciousness, metacognitive awareness). The mediation of activity across intrinsic and extrinsic brain networks.

Metta. A Pali word (pronounced meh-tuh) that means loving-kindness, gentle friendship, also known as maitri, is a Buddhist practice for generating loving-kindness and is said to be first taught by the Buddha as an antidote to fear. Metta helps develop your capacity for an open and loving heart. It is traditionally offered along with other meditations that enrich compassion, joy in the happiness of others, and mental calmness. Loving-kindness practice leads to the development of concentration, fearlessness, happiness, and a greater ability to love.

Mindful Attention Training (MAT). A mindfulness practice used to increase attention.

Mindfulness. This is paying attention to what you are doing in the moment without judgment. Attention to the present moment; mindfulness is a way of bringing meditation into all your daily activities. In mindfulness, you let thoughts move in and out of your mind on their own while breathing gently. You should treat each idea without judgment.

Mindfulness-Based Stress Reduction (MBSR). One of the first contemporary mindfulness practices developed in the late 1970s to reduce stress.

Movement. Any time you move your body and shift your posture. Movement shifts the activity of your autonomic nervous system, which in turn shifts your emotions and your mood.

Monkey Mind. According to Buddhist principles, the "monkey mind" is a term that refers to being unsettled, restless, capricious, whimsical, fanciful, inconstant, confused, indecisive, or uncontrollable. In more practical terms, it's the voice inside your head.

Mudra. The position you must put your hands in during meditation (pronounced mu-draa). The Sanskrit word, which means "seal," is a hand gesture or whole-body gesture that is used in prayer or meditation.

Nadi. This is the Sanskrit term meaning "conduit," and it refers to one of 72,000 or more subtle channels along or through which your life force (prana) circulates (pronounced naa-Dii).

Nadi–shodhana. A Sanskrit term meaning "channel cleansing" (pronounced naa-Dii sho-dhuh-nun). This refers to the practice of purifying the channels of subtle energy, especially by using breath control (pranayama). It is also the name of the practice of alternate nostril breathing.

Namaste. Namaste is a salutation in the Hindu culture (pronounced nah–mah–stay) to express a polite and peaceful hello or goodbye. Namaste translates to "the divine light within me salutes the divine light within you." Namaskar is a similar salutation. You may hear it as you exit yoga class or after an encounter or meeting with a friend. This word can be divided into three sections: Nama means "bow." In this gesture, you bow forward with both hands together. Holding both hands together closest to the heart chakra indicates prayer position. Moving hands to the center facing the teacher (or yogi) acknowledges and thanks the teacher for the practice.

Om. The original mantra symbolizing the ultimate reality claimed to be the most powerful mantra (pronounced ohm). It is a prefix to many mantras. If used alone, the spelling is Aum (pronounced as aa-uu-eemm). It is said to amplify what it precedes and is considered the sound of the universe.

Padmasana. Seated lotus posture (pronounced pad-Maa-sana).

Prana. It is a Sanskrit term meaning vitality, life force, or energy. (pronounced praa-naa). In other practices, it is called chi or qi. This is the universal source of energy, vitalizing and infusing all matter. Prana integrates into subatomic particles and atoms, which become the basic building blocks of all matter manifesting in the physical world. Every molecule, cell, and atom is an extension of prana, just as waves are extensions of the sea that lies beneath it. Prana is also the life force that flows in all living forms and performs vital functions.

Pranayama. It is a Sanskrit term that means breath control or extension (pronounced praa-naa-yaa-muh). It is practiced by conscious inhalation, exhalation, and retention.

Rooted / Grounded. You "root" to ground yourself and to find strength. It is essential to ground/root yourself by tuning in to your root chakra at the beginning and throughout your practice. Your root (muladhara) chakra is what leads you to feel safe and secure. This is your foundation and represents your connection to the earth and your sense of "rootedness" in life. If the root chakra were in nature, it would be the soil where seeds are planted. It's the "ground floor" of the chakra system and lays the foundation for expansion in your life.

Sankalpa. Also, "setting an intention" (pronounced Sun-Kul-Pa). It is a Sanskrit word that means respect, desire, or intention. It is like an idea that forms in the mind and takes root in the heart until it is actualized. In the yoga tradition, before meditation or yoga practice, or even at the start of your day, you can make a resolution called a Sankalpa. This is a brief statement your repeat to create the life you are meant to embrace. When your mind is calm and quiet, your Sankalpa plants a seed in your soul.

Sat Nam. Sat means truth in the ancient Sikh language called Gurmukhi (pronounced s-uh-t-n-aa-m). Nam means name. Together, Sat Nam essentially translates into something more profound: "I am truth" or "Truth is my essence."

Savasana, or Shavasana. It is the Sanskrit name for a restorative asana (pronounced sha-vA-sa-na) and a key component of asana practice in almost every yoga tradition. It is most commonly used at the end of a sequence to relax and integrate.

Self–compassion. It is the practice of being kind and understanding toward ourselves when we suffer, fail, or feel inadequate, rather than ignoring our pain or beating ourselves up with self–criticism.

Shanti. When you chant, "Om shanti shanti shanti," it's an invocation of peace (pronounced shaan-tee). In Hindu and Buddhist traditions, one chants shanti three times to represent peace in body, speech, and mind.

Softening Into. This arises through the skill of abandoning participation through deeply relaxing 'into' physical and mental resistance.

Third Eye. A tool for sensing realities beyond your own. This is the sixth chakra and is said to be located in the center of your head, parallel to the middle of your eyebrows.

Touch. The power of touch soothes the nervous system and restores a sense of safety and trust in the moment. Warm, safe touch activates the release of oxytocin, the brain's direct and immediate antidote to the stress hormone cortisol.

Tune In. It is often done at the beginning of meditation practice but can be done at any time during your practice. This is the act of pausing and focusing your attention on your breathing. While you do this, you check in with yourself and sense how you feel in your body, thoughts, and emotions. You can sense if you are feeling grounded (rooted) or distracted, if you are having good thoughts or negative ones, and sense how present you are in that moment. In this process, you focus on where it's easiest to feel the sensations of your breath flowing in and out—your nostrils, your throat, and in the rise and fall of your chest or belly. Often (but not always), a Tibetan bowl sound or chime sound is used in meditation to signal the time to tune in at the beginning of meditation practice.

Vipassana. This Pali term means to "see clearly" (pronounced vi-pash-ana). This refers to the practice of insight meditation: moment–to–moment mindfulness. Through careful and sustained observation, you directly experience the ever-changing flow of the mind-body process. This awareness lets you fully accept the pleasure and pain, fear and joy, sadness and happiness that life inevitably brings. As insight deepens, the cultivation of greater calmness and peace rises up in the face of change. Wisdom and compassion increasingly become the guiding principles of your life.

Yama. A Sanskrit word meaning to "reign in" or "control (pronounced ya-maa)." A yama is a guideline for social behavior, virtue, self–restraint, a rule of conduct, or social grace. Yamas are one of the eight limbs of yoga. The five yamas ask practitioners to avoid lying, stealing, violence, wasting energy, and possessiveness.

Yoga Nidra. Yogic sleep in modern usage is a state of consciousness between waking and sleeping, typically induced by a guided meditation (pronounced yoga-nih-draah).

Yogi. A person is undertaking the spiritual path of awakening; a meditator (pronounced yo-gi).

Zazen. The Japanese Buddhist meditation technique practiced in the Zen Buddhist tradition (pronounced zah-zen). In Zazen, being aware of your breath is recommended. Most zazen practitioners do this by counting breaths using different techniques. When the mind wanders, which often happens, you gently turn your attention back to the breath.

Zen. A school of Mahayana Buddhism with its roots in Japan. It's a practice that emphasizes the attainment of enlightenment and the personal expression of direct insight through Zazen and interaction with an accomplished teacher.

THE BIGGEST MYTH ABOUT MEDITATION

The Myth: *The goal of meditation is to clear your mind to achieve a thoughtless state.*

The most pervasive myth about meditation is that it requires stopping all thoughts. You know that every time you try to push your thoughts away, it's usually ineffective to try to eliminate all thoughts. In fact, the more you try to "stop thinking," the more your thoughts persist!

Thoughts themselves are not the problem. It's your relationship to the thought that is the issue. We can get lost in our thoughts. We fight with them, react to them, suppress them or act them out. This wastes precious energy, tortures your mind, and can leave you exhausted!

Stopping thinking and thoughts is not the objective of meditation. The aim is to be more aware of thoughts so that our thoughts don't control us.

The mindset you come to meditation with is how you will train your mind. Meditating with strain, anxiety, and tension reinforces your nervous system's impatience and anxiety. If you meditate with gentleness, patience, and curiosity towards yourself, you'll strengthen those qualities.

THE OBJECTIVE OF MEDITATION

The fundamental objective of meditation is to create a "space" between you and what is your body and mind and to enjoy the process. Meditation is about opening your heart, connecting to spirit, training the mind, and understanding the nature of experience itself. For some people who are used to having a set "end goal" in mind, this is often not easy.

If there is any other "objective" of meditation practice, it would be to develop a more profound sense of mindfulness. There is even a specific type of meditation known as mindfulness meditation. Mindfulness meditation is focused on helping you learn to live with whatever you may be feeling at that particular moment. When those feelings and thoughts come up for you, mindfulness helps you acknowledge and accept them without analysis or judgment.

Remember it this way: meditation is the practice, and mindfulness is the result.

Like laws of physics govern the natural world, specific laws rule our inner life. When we don't understand these elemental truths, we struggle against them, straining relationships and making complicated things in life more challenging.

The more we understand these laws, the less we will struggle. The less we struggle, the more we experience a feeling of natural peace and clarity that does not depend on external conditions. We realize that we ultimately can't control things. Instead, we find freedom in learning to see clearly and letting go of rigid expectations about how things "should be."

Meditation provides space for us to study how the heart and mind work. The more clearly we observe direct experience, the more we understand that everything changes at a deep, intuitive level. Nothing in life is completely solid or dependable.

The secret of meditation is that it teaches us that it's not about what happens but how we relate to the things that happen to us.

SPIRITUALITY AND MEDITATION

Meditation does not have to be spiritual or religious, but it can be if you want it to be.

For as long as history has been recorded, meditation has been a part of every religion. If you study meditation more deeply, you will discover its religious origins. Today, meditation is quite mainstream, and its religious roots have been diluted for Western practitioners.

Over the last half-century, meditation practices adapted from various religious traditions have become widely accepted as helpful for managing stress. The mental health community has increasingly used meditation as a treatment method.

Meditation appeals to many people because it does not need a god, sacred texts, or a ritual, and it doesn't promise salvation. Meditation is simply connecting with your innermost self through the most natural thing you know how to do – breathing! And this can be a completely secular experience. Secular meditation and mindfulness allow us to access the many benefits of meditation free from religious sectarianism.

Meditation is natural to humans, and in times past, meditation came easily to us. Unfortunately, most humans have lost touch with what it means to be present in our modern world. Listening to the sound of water gurgling in a stream, sitting in a field, watching the grass wave and hearing it brush together in the wind, or observing and listening to the birds happily chirping around us were all things we used to take a lot more time to do. Those activities have meditative qualities to them.

Secular meditation is a term we use to describe modern mindfulness

It has its roots in Mindfulness Based Stress Reduction, an evidence-based practice developed by Professor of Medicine Jon Kabat-Zinn in 1979. It emerged as a way to define meditation practice and techniques that you can practice without reference to any religious traditions.

As you begin your meditation practice, you may feel the urge to go deeper and want to discover more about your spiritual self. This is achievable through regular spiritual meditation. Spiritual meditation is a meditation practice you undertake with the desire to connect with a higher power. Unlike other meditation forms, spiritual meditation is about much more than stress reduction or relaxation. When you practice spiritual meditation specifically, you can get access to various emotions and discover your spiritual path. You should not force this practice, and you shouldn't attempt to rush into it.

In spiritual meditation, the aim is to merge your sense of 'I' into the infinite. You focus on a spiritual idea that is greater than yourself, and your mind is directed towards that spiritual idea. The simplest way to think of this is to think of infinite love, peace, happiness, or an entity embodying that. You may call it God, Source Energy, The Universe, Bhagavan, Adonai, Akal Purakh, Khu, or many names for a higher power, but the name is not important. What is essential is to remember that this infinite love is surrounding us and inside us. As we meditate on this infinite and beautiful idea, our mind is transformed into pure consciousness, which has no boundary.

A few examples of spiritual meditation in major religious traditions include:

- Christian contemplative prayer
- Hindu japa mala and mantra meditation
- Jewish Kabbalah, the ethic of meditation mysticism in

Abulafia and other Ecstatic Kabbalists
- Loving-kindness or metta meditation in Buddhism
- Marananussati bhavana or reflection on one's mortality in Theravada Buddhism
- Sufi dhikr or remembrance of God
- Trance states in Shamanistic traditions
- Zazen meditation in Zen Buddhism

Spirituality has multiple definitions, most of which differ on a point of context. Despite the differences, spiritual meditation is used globally in countless religions and cultures. People in different traditions worldwide employ spiritual meditation to connect to the divine. Spirituality means knowing yourself and connecting to a higher power using different methods. Prayers, thoughts, mantras, and other rituals are forms of meditation, and meditation is the doorway to spirituality. The foundation of spiritual meditation is using intention to get insight into your life purpose and meaning.

WHY YOU SHOULD MEDITATE

Not only does meditation help you cognitively, spiritually, psychologically, and emotionally, but it can also make you physically healthier.

The traditional context of meditation is self–discovery and deepening understanding of life's sacred and mystical forces.

People come to meditation practice for different purposes. One of the top reasons people meditate is for health reasons. Spending even a few minutes meditating can regulate your heartbeat and restore your calm and inner peace. Anyone can practice meditation. Meditation is simple and inexpensive; it doesn't require special equipment and can be done anywhere.

Thousands of studies have shown the indisputable effects of meditation. It helps manage many physical ailments and conditions related to stress. Increasingly, therapists use meditation to model healthier ways to relate to the mind and overcome anxiety and negative thoughts. Meditation is powerful enough to rewire your brain. Many studies using MRI (magnetic resonance imaging) and EEG have shown that a regular meditation practice can rewire the neural patterns in the brain.

Often, when you feel overwhelmed by life, meditation is a refuge. Meditation practice helps you create space from the chaos in your head, aids in relaxation, and refreshes your perspective.

Mindfulness meditation is now very popular in the workplace as a way to prepare for meetings, improve teamwork, improve focus, handle criticism, and prepare for presentations.

Here are some other reasons to begin a mediation practice:

It can help you be successful in life and increase self-awareness: Meditation causes changes in brain waves that improve the brain's functionality. This helps you gain clarity and focus to be more successful in your life. Self–awareness is the process of connecting with your true self. Meditation enables you to focus in the moment without life's distractions. It also helps you tap into your subconscious mind, leaving you still and calm.

It may help you sleep better: If you struggle with sleep, meditation has many benefits, like enhanced REM (rapid eye movement) sleep and increased melatonin levels. It is proven that mindfulness meditation helps improve sleep. During mindfulness meditation, you focus on your breathing and stop thinking about the past and future, only focusing on the present. Once you have let go and are fully relaxed, you are in a better state for a good night's sleep. By slowing down and observing the activity of your mind, you can recognize and understand your ingrained patterns of behavior and thought. You can recognize deep or yet unknown motivations within. Through regular meditation, you can train your attention to focus on the most important things to you, your goals, and your visions.

It helps to eliminate stress eating: Meditation can help prevent overeating by retraining the mind and allowing space for mindfulness so you don't turn to food to calm stress.

It may improve concentration: Meditation may help you get more work done by giving you a clear mind and helping to improve your concentration, memory, and focus.

It may improve your love life and relationships with others: By learning to recognize and be with your own emotions and the emotions of others, you'll more easily experience lasting harmony in your relationships.

It helps you manage negative thoughts: Meditation helps you gain awareness of your mind enabling you to recognize negative thoughts and thought patterns and say, "those thoughts are not me." Becoming less identified with our thoughts helps those thoughts lose power. Deep mediation can allow you access to a part of yourself that feels infinite. Spending time resting in this space is wonderfully positive. It gives you confidence and gratitude for the intrinsic goodness of life.

It can help with pain management and healing: Meditation and mindfulness can significantly improve pain symptoms and quality of life in cases of chronic pain. MRIs show reductions in pain induced cerebral blood flow during meditation sessions.

It can help reduce anxiety: Focusing on all the terrible things that might happen to us but often don't takes us away from the present and causes our bodies a lot of stress. Meditation helps reduce anxiety and is proven to help those with generalized anxiety disorder.

It aids in relaxation and rejuvenation: Relaxing your body and mind with meditation helps you stay centered when encountering everyday stressors. Practicing meditation causes the relaxation response, the opposite of the fight–or–flight response, which happens to our bodies when we get stressed. The relaxation response alleviates anxiety and positively affects heart rate, blood pressure, and brain activity. Meditation also helps rejuvenate you; it lets you relieve any negativity that may be weighing you down.

It is effective for stress reduction: It is a fact that meditation reduces employee stress and burnout. It's no secret that famous artists, Wall Street executives, world-famous entrepreneurs, and tech wizards are some of the most prominent meditation advocates for managing stress.

BENEFITS OF MEDITATION

When you meditate, you get rid of the information overload that builds up every day and contributes to your anxiety, stress, and lack of clarity.

Research on the effects of meditation on the brain has been coming in steadily for many years now. Studies are being released almost every week that prove new benefits of meditation and are confirmed with fMRI (functional magnetic resonance imaging) or EEG (electroencephalogram). Meditation seems to have a fantastic variety of neurological benefits. These include changes in grey matter volume, reduced activity in your brain's "me" centers, and enhanced connectivity between your brain regions.

The emotional and physical benefits of meditation can include:

- Aids in sleep
- Focusing on the present
- Gaining a new perspective on stressful situations
- Improves self–image
- Increases a sense of positivity
- Increases gratitude
- Increases kindness
- Increasing attention span
- Increasing imagination and creativity
- Increasing patience and tolerance
- Increasing self–awareness
- Less anxiety
- Promotes overall emotional health
- Promotes deep relaxation
- Reducing negative emotions
- Reduction in stress levels

For those with medical conditions exacerbated by stress, meditation may also be helpful to you.

While a growing body of scientific research supports the health benefits of meditation, some researchers believe it's not yet possible to conclude all the potential benefits of meditation. The study of its effects is ongoing.

Keeping that in mind, some research suggests that meditation may help people manage symptoms of conditions such as:

- Addiction
- Age-Related Memory Loss
- Anxiety
- Asthma
- Blood Circulation
- Blood Cortisol
- Blood Pressure
- Cancer
- Chronic Pain
- Depression
- Heart Disease
- High Blood Pressure
- Irritable Bowel Syndrome
- Panic Attacks
- Perspiration
- Post Traumatic Stress Disorder
- Respiratory Issues
- Sleep Problems
- Tension Headaches

HOW LONG YOU SHOULD MEDITATE

The best way to approach time is to start small, build up slowly and find your own personal sweet spot. For some people, this sweet spot is 10 minutes, and for others, it's 60 minutes. The most important thing is to be realistic and start where you are.

Most importantly, you should choose a realistic, practical, repeatable, and enjoyable length of time.

Consistent meditation is the key to making the practice work for you.

When you begin, try meditating for 1 to 5 minutes a day. Start with just 1 minute a day, sit in silence, listen to your breath, and just be present. When you can sit still and relax for that long, bump it up to 5 minutes then 10 minutes. After that, increase your time every day as you get comfortable with the practice – find your sweet spot. This approach will help you commit to your meditation practice without creating too much pressure on yourself, reducing stress levels, and making meditation more accessible for beginners.

The important thing is to be consistent. You are trying to establish a new habit for yourself so keeping it simple is the best approach.

After a few weeks, you can start to evaluate the impact and results of your meditation practice. Because we are all different, there isn't a "right amount of time" to meditate. But it's scientifically proven that the more time you invest in practice, the better the result you will experience.

10 STEPS TO START A MEDITATION PRACTICE YOU CAN STICK TO

As mentioned previously, the simplest way to get into a regular meditation practice is to start with 1–5 minutes per day. Set aside time every day to get used to the practice, and as you get used to it, you can extend your meditation time to find your sweet spot.

Experiment with different types of meditation to see what resonates most with you. Later in this guide, I will outline the most common types of meditation. I suggest starting with focused meditations like breathing, counting, mantra, or guided meditation.

10 Simple Steps to Start Your Meditation Practice

Meditation does not have to be complex. It's really, really simple. This is how you can do it:

1. Set your time and place
2. Experiment with different meditation techniques each session using readily available resources
3. Get comfortable
4. Sit tall
5. Start with 30 seconds or 1 minute
6. Just keep breathing
7. Be really kind to yourself
8. Notice your excuses
9. Commit to daily practice – practice makes perfect
10. Use a meditation journal (awesome, you already are!)

I recommend that you use a straight-forward approach. Unless you are practicing a particular form of yogic meditation, breathing meditation, or pranayama, allow your breath to be natural, whether you are counting it or not. It's helpful to take a few deep breaths at the beginning of your practice to let go of stress and infuse your blood with oxygen.

After a few weeks, you can evaluate the impact and results of your meditation practice and techniques. As mentioned in this guide in the next section, there are many different meditation types. Experiment with them and see which ones you love the most. There isn't a "right amount of time" to meditate, nor is there a "right type of meditation technique" to practice. We are all different. The right meditation technique and your sweet spot for time to meditate will be unique and may change as you practice more often. The more time you invest in your meditation practice, the more results you will see.

HOW TO SET A MEDITATION
INTENTION WITH EXAMPLES

Intentions are key to any mindful practice, such as yoga or meditation. You can use an intention to anchor yourself during your practice because it's normal for your mind to wander.

The expression "set an intention" is easy enough to understand, but what does "intention" in the context of meditation really mean? If you don't fully understand the purpose and effect of intentions, the use can seem difficult to understand.

Intentions play a vital role in connecting the mind and body. Setting an intention is activating your receptiveness. If you go out into your day and have no intention of how you want your day to go, you're getting on a random path with no direction. Having no plan can be great sometimes because you're allowing Universal energy to direct your steps. But if you know that you want to get somewhere specific, the power of setting an intention will help you get there.

Setting a meditation intention is like plotting a map of where you want to go with your meditation. It outlines what you want your meditation to do, include and achieve.

If you focus your mind on a specific intention during your meditation, you bring that focus to the front of your heart, mind, and spirit. This helps manifest that intention to reality.

Please understand that an intention is not a mantra. While the two terms are at times used interchangeably, they are different. An intention is about how you want to feel during your practice. A mantra is a sound or phrase that you repeat in your meditation. An intention is more than just a single word or phrase.

If you use intentions in your mediation practice, your sessions will be more focused, and you may find you get more out of them. You can set an intention ahead of time or wait until you are ready to meditate to set your intention. Sometimes sitting comfortably, taking several deep breaths in and out, and allowing the intention to come to you is a great start. You can see what comes to you at that moment and what you need to focus on during your session.

The intention you set for meditation is essential as it will direct how your meditation session goes for you. When it comes to you deciding what intention to set, a solid place to start is by asking yourself a few questions, like:

- What matters the most to me?
- What parts of my body need extra love today?
- What do I want to let go of?
- What am I the most grateful for in my life?
- What things about myself make me proud?
- Are there any emotions I need to pay more attention to today?
- Are there any parts of myself I need to forgive or release today?
- What do I desire to do, build or nurture to make my life happier?
- What do my mind and body feel like when I am my happiest self?
- Who do I want to forgive?

These self-probing questions can help you put your intentions into context and decide which intention will work best for you.

Remember that these should be intentions, not goals! Your goals will inform what intentions you set for yourself, but you need to remind yourself that there is a difference between an intention and a goal. When you set your intention, there is no "result" demanded, and you should go easy on your heart and soul. Setting an intention for your meditation will create a map for your meditation and help it be more successful and productive. You will start to get much more out of your practice and out of your life when the right intentions guide your meditations.

Here are a few examples of meditation intentions that you can use to go in the right direction. You can modify these meditation intentions to fit your life and your goals.

- I intend to release all that is not mine to carry.
- I intend to be open to prosperity.
- I intend to make self-care a priority every day.
- I intend to be open to receiving and giving love.
- I intend to easily manifest happiness in my life.
- I intend not to allow negativity to penetrate my heart.
- I intend to find harmony in my life.
- I intend to set a positive example for others.
- I intend to allow myself to experience vulnerability.
- I intend to forgive those who have hurt me.
- I intend to do something kind for someone else today.
- I intend to embrace change.
- I intend to make well-grounded decisions for myself.
- I intend to love unconditionally.

These don't have to be your intentions specifically, but these are solid examples of intentions you can use during your meditation.

HOW TO FIND MEDITATIONS

The most immediate way to find meditations is to search on YouTube, Google, or an app such as Insight Timer or Headspace. There you can find meditations by type and length to suit your needs as you begin your meditation practice.

PeacelandHaven.com has links to some amazing meditation Channels on YouTube and sites to source meditations and download apps. Refer to the last page of this book under "Additional Resources". You can also search on Facebook for a meditation group to see about connecting with people globally or locally to meditate with or share meditations.

Many meditation books on Amazon.com or at your local bookstore have meditation scripts that you can read for self-guided meditation.

If you are into community meditation, the best thing to do is search for local yoga studios that have meditation classes or events. Group, in-person meditation is a beautiful experience. I highly recommend that you try it at least once to see how that energy feels for you personally.

HOW TO USE THIS MEDITATION JOURNAL

Included after this guide is a 90 Day Meditation Journal segment. The format I have created for you in this journal includes 1 page per session to record many aspects of your daily meditation practice, including:

Date and time of the session - record the date and time you meditated.

Location - note where you meditated for that session.

Duration - note how long you meditated.

Meditation Method - note which meditation style you used (affirmation, guided, body scan, movement, etc.).

Mantra/Affirmation - write it here if you used a mantra or affirmation.

Meditation Position - note the position you meditated in during that session.

Meditation Intention - note what your meditation intention was. An intention shouldn't be confused with a goal. It's not something you attach an expectation or evaluation to. It is something you want to align within your practice. It's an aim, a purpose, or an attitude you'd be proud to commit to. Intentions come from your heart; they are not the tangible "increase sales by 35%" or "get a raise" type of goal that you set at work. Meditation intentions are heart-driven and evoke feeling and purpose, like "practice being non-judgmental of myself and others," "send compassion out into the world," "open my heart," and "let go of fear." Setting an intention is a way to bring your heart and mind into alignment.

Feelings and perceptions - note what feelings came up for you during your meditation practice. What did you become aware of with your senses as you practiced?

Insights or realizations - note down any understandings, a-ha moments, or revelations you had during your practice.

I am grateful for - list a few things you are grateful for. Daily gratitude practice opens your heart.

I am working towards - note what you are working towards in your meditation practice. This could be a longer session, more deep breathing, or trying out a new asana or meditation method.

I am letting go of - note what you are letting go of today and keep that in mind as you carry on with the rest of your daily activities.

Additional Notes - note anything else that came up for you in your meditation session or use this space for a mini-journaling session.

Journal Page - use this page along with the suggested journal prompts to explore mindful journaling.

You don't have to use each section, though it is recommended to do so. You can use only the sections that resonate with you.

Keeping your journal should be a rewarding, positive, and enjoyable experience. This journal provides an entry point to meditation journaling. Later on, once you develop your practice, you can use a lined notebook to write freely about your meditation experience or purchase a meditation journal. Putting a pen down to paper enforces retention much more than typing on a phone or computer. Also, when you're sitting down and writing by hand, it limits distraction.

Typing into a device is usually not as beneficial for most people.

30 MEDITATION JOURNAL PROMPTS

The act of mindful journaling has compelling benefits — it is an excellent meditative practice. When you write in your meditation journal, your mind will fully engage with your writing. This forces your brain to slow down to organize your thoughts better and consider the big picture. In the flow of your meditation journaling, past regrets and future worries lose their power. You, your mind, and your pen and paper become one in the present moment.

Top reasons to journal:

- Journaling can be used to increase positive thoughts.
- Journaling can be used to decrease negative thoughts.
- Journaling helps sharpen your focus.
- Journaling can be done anywhere.
- Journaling focuses your attention inward.
- Journaling is easy to do.
- Journaling has little or no cost.
- Journaling can be done at any age.

You can use the lined journal page on the journal pages at the end of this guide to try out some journaling. The space provided is limited, so you can use an additional piece of paper or purchase a lined notebook or meditation journal if you need more space.

Here are some example prompts to get you started:

1. I reflect on the people in my life who have made me feel loved and supported. I feel grateful for...

2. Today I sit quietly for a few moments and observe my thoughts as they float by in my mind. I don't

judge them. I just watch and notice. What does observation reveal to me about my thoughts?

3. I am grateful for the great conversations I have had in my life. As I reflect on the conversations I have shared with friends, families, and colleagues. I am grateful for...

4. I am mindful of my health and my body. As I reflect on the times when I have enjoyed good health. I am grateful for...

5. I have many experiences in my life that have taught me so much. If I could relive an experience in my life, it would be this experience because it taught me...

6. I have gratitude for the physical space I am in. These are the five things I love most about my physical space...

7. When I take time to meditate and scan my physical body, these are the things I feel in my physical body...

8. Health is wealth, and I am taking care of myself. These are the ways I am looking after my health...

9. Sometimes bad days happen. I handle a bad day by...

10. I am great at my job/studies. I consider this to be my most significant professional/academic success...

11. As I sit quietly, I notice each breath I take, following the intake of air through my nose and into my lungs and the slow exhalation as I release the air through my nose. As I repeat this mindful breathing for several minutes, I notice my body...

12. I am excited to be learning more about meditation daily. These are the five things I have learned about meditation that have helped me the most...

13. I am aware of my strengths and skills, which have helped me on the path to where I am today. I feel grateful for...

14. I notice that I sometimes lie to myself. The biggest lie I tell myself is...

15. When I quiet my mind and connect with my true essence, I feel a sense of connection to my journey on this earth. I am most thankful for these five things in my earth journey so far...

16. When I feel anxious in meditation or in life, I do these three things to calm down...

17. In today's meditation, some emotions came up for me. Those emotions were...

18. Sometimes when I meditate, critical thoughts come up for me. The top three inner criticisms I hear in my head are...

19. When I quiet my mind and feel peace, I smile. These are the top 5 things that make me smile during meditation...

20. I notice I procrastinate sometimes. The top 3 things I procrastinate about are...

21. As I grow stronger in my mind with regular meditation practice, I am becoming more aware of my unique emotional strengths. These unique emotional strengths are (i.e. empathy, compassion, kindness, etc.)...

22. I notice in my meditative state a sense of control being developed. This sense of control makes me feel more...

23. I am developing more compassion and a desire to communicate with people in a way that brings clarity. Lately, I have been doing these things to clarify my communication with others...

24. Today a strong emotion came up for me in my meditation. I realize that the emotion I felt needs this from me...

25. I understand that the body and mind need time to rest and recharge. My meditation practice helps me do this. These are some other self-care things I am doing to help rest and recharge myself...

26. I am learning to be proud of myself. Today what made me most proud of myself was...

27. I notice that I can be a bit hard on myself sometimes. If I spoke to myself as if I were a small child, I would say to myself...

28. In my meditation today, I set an intention. I set this intention because...

29. Feeling happy is fantastic, and I love how meditation allows me space to feel happy. Right now, what has me feeling most happy is...

30. I enjoy eating food and am being more mindful when I eat. Today when I ate food, I noticed it did this to my body and emotions...

TYPES OF MEDITATION

Meditation is a catch-all term for the many ways to train the mind and achieve a relaxed state of being. There are many types of meditation and relaxation methods that have meditation components. All share the same goal of achieving inner peace. Once you have read some of the types of meditation, you can search for them using Google, YouTube, or your favorite meditation app. Try a few out and see which ones are your favorites.

Some ways to meditate include:

Affirmation Meditation – Affirmation meditation is the practice of positive thinking and self–empowerment. An affirmation is a conscious thought that tends to be positive and powerful and aims to support you somehow. Using affirmations can be a great way to harness your strengths, focus on the good in life, elevate your mood and create a more positive reality for yourself. Meditation with affirmations is like bathing in positivity! You'll be deeply relaxed and absorbed in the affirmations as they penetrate your mind as you practice. An affirmation is anything repeated out loud or in your thoughts that registers in your subconscious mind, which is open to the positive directions that your affirmations provide. Effective affirmations are positive, personal, specific, and in the present tense.

Body Scan or Progressive Relaxation – A simple progressive relaxation technique. Taking your mind within and connecting with the muscles and muscle groups can bring about deep relaxation and a sense of peace and stillness.

Chakra Meditation – Chakra is a Sanskrit word that means wheel or cycle. In spiritual disciplines such as yoga, the chakras are considered to be wheel-like energy centers that are not physically discernable but belong to the subtle spiritual body and connect it to the physical one. The seven main chakras are located along the spine from the sacrum at the bottom up to the crown at the top of the head. Chakra meditation is a general term for any type of meditation that aims to clear blocked chakras and use the power of these energy centers located throughout the body. You can use them to promote calm and relaxation and encourage spiritual awakening. This is a form of meditation that targets your unaligned or blocked chakras. You can choose to use chakra color meditation, a meditation on energy, or a meditation on an individual chakra.

Focused Meditation – Focused meditation, also called focused attention meditation (FAM), is choosing one object to pay attention to, such as sound, sensation, or object, rather than trying to achieve a clear mind without a central point of focus. When your mind wanders, it allows you to bring attention to that chosen object.

Kundalini Meditation – Kundalini meditation is an active and energizing practice that is part of Kundalini yoga. It clears the path for the ascent of Kundalini energy from the base of the spine. This is done via visualization, repetition of mantras, and breathing, which helps move the energy at the bottom of the spine (also known as the root chakra) that needs to be released through the body's seven chakras and then out through the crown chakra above the head.

Loving–Kindness Meditation – Loving-kindness meditation is a form of meditation that focuses on cultivating feelings of goodwill, kindness, and compassion. Its Pali name, Metta Bhavana, or loving-kindness meditation, is a method of developing compassion. It's a type of Buddhist meditation. Anyone can adapt and practice it, regardless of religion or belief system. Metta means "love," in the unromantic, unconditional sense, and Bhavana means "cultivation" or "development." The key to loving-kindness meditation is understanding that the feelings cultivated should be inclusive and undiscriminating. Nothing is expected in return, and it is considered the purest form of love. The practice is said to soften the heart and mind, opening you up to experiencing feelings of deep warmth and affection for yourself and others.

Mantra Meditation – Mantra is a Sanskrit term, with "man" meaning "mind" and "tra" meaning "release." A mantra is a syllable, word, or phrase repeated during meditation. Meditation mantras are words or phrases you can sing, chant, hum, whisper, or repeat silently in your mind as you meditate. Most mantra meditation techniques have two essential components: mindfulness meditation and mantra recitation or chanting. While this ancient practice is known to have Buddhist and Hindu roots, forms of "sacred word" recitation exist in various spiritual traditions, including Judeo–Christian, and Shamanic. Nowadays, mantra practice is also gaining popularity in secular mindfulness practice.

Mindfulness Meditation – Mindfulness meditation combines the concepts of mindfulness and meditation. When you are mindful, you focus on being intensely aware of what you're sensing and feeling in the moment, without interpretation or judgment. Mindfulness keeps you from overreacting or getting overwhelmed in stressful situations. Mindfulness utilizes breathing methods, guided imagery, and other practices to relax the body and mind and help reduce stress.

Movement Meditation – Movement meditation focuses on the movements of the body rather than the goal of the movement to provide a path to contemplation. Movement refers to meditation practices or exercises that energize the body and mind through calm and purposeful breathing or movement. Movement meditation allows you to experience the body's sensations as well as gravity and energy as embodied phenomena. Movement meditation is not your usual meditation where you sit still and focus on your breath. Instead, you move through various positions at a mindful and slow pace. Examples of this style are Walking Meditation, Qigong, and Tai Chi.

Spiritual Meditation – Spiritual Meditation is an experience that transports you beyond any limited identities and labels to the truth of who you truly are. Traditions worldwide employ spiritual meditation as a way to connect to the divine. Spiritual meditation makes you realize the eternal truth and let go of all that has and will happen. The desire to practice spiritual meditation comes from an innate longing to see and think beyond the chaotic world.

Transcendental Meditation – Transcendental Meditation (TM) is an ancient Vedic tradition that originated in India and inspired the Transcendental Meditation Movement led by Maharishi Mahesh Yogi. In TM, you learn how to effortlessly transcend — go beyond the surface level of your awareness. This state of deep inner silence involves silently repeating a mantra for 15–20 minutes a day. It is usually done sitting with the eyes closed. The official TM training program requires specialized 7–step training from a certified instructor. Your teacher gifts you with a particular mantra passed down by Maharishi. The mantra is usually a Sanskrit word or sound you repeat to yourself to rest your attention and used as the vehicle to help the mind settle down.

Yoga Nidra – Yoga nidra, or yogic sleep in modern usage, is a state of consciousness between waking and sleeping, typically induced by a guided meditation. If you're looking for deep relaxation, this form of yoga can help.

Zen Meditation – Zen meditation, also known as Zazen, is a meditation technique rooted in the Buddhist tradition that new and seasoned meditators can practice. The goal of Zen meditation is to regulate attention. Zen meditation provides insight into how the mind works. It focuses on posture: open shoulders, upright spine, soft belly, and on the ground (chair or cushion). You follow the breath one inhalation and one exhalation at a time. Each time a thought arises, you just don't follow the thought and return to the breath.

35 MEDITATION TIPS

1. **Just get started.**
   Don't think that you can't meditate. Meditation is something that everyone can do at any time and anywhere. If you are worried that you don't understand what it's about, don't worry, nobody does initially! Just start. The moment you do, you will begin to reap all of the benefits of meditation.

2. **Keep it simple.**
   Don't worry about whether you're doing it the "right way" or the "wrong way." Lots of thoughts will naturally come up in your mind. This can feel overwhelming. Don't get discouraged. Just keep it simple by constantly returning to the breath.

3. **Prepare.**
   Whether you want to meditate in the morning or the evening after a busy day at work, give yourself a few minutes to prepare. Preparing well ensures a more profound and pleasurable experience. Setting your attention on a single point of focus may help. You can use a candle, an image, or bring your attention to one of your chakras or one of your body parts. Keep your eyes closed and focus on your intention, resting the mind there.

4. **Switch to airplane mode.**
   Put your phone in airplane mode. This is one of the most crucial meditation preparations of modern times! There's no better way to kill the vibe of a fantastic meditation session than by leaving your phone on and getting a text, notification, or phone call in the middle of your blissed-out meditation session. Turn your phone off or put it on airplane mode when you prepare to meditate.

5. **Choose a time to meditate, and stay with it.**
   When you schedule a time of day and place to meditate, it is easier to establish a habit, and you'll be more likely to do it daily. You will be able to relax into your practice more quickly. The best time to meditate will vary from person to person, depending on your preferences, schedule, and lifestyle.

6. **Create a designated space to meditate.**
   The stillness around you can help you find peace inside yourself. If possible, meditate somewhere calm, quiet, and not too cluttered. Somewhere quiet and familiar can help train the mind and body to feel more comfortable and allow you to transition into meditation more easily. Setting up a comfortable environment will help create the right vibe for your practice. You can return to the same place to practice daily.

7. **Build a habit.**
   There is great power in creating habits. A simple tip is to make meditation a habit by doing it daily if possible. Many of us find excuses not to practice. If we feel a need to get many other things done before meditating, it's just procrastination. Building an excellent meditation habit requires effort and consistency. Your daily routine will start to fit around your meditation practice.

8. **Find the most comfortable position for yourself.**
   Forget stereotypical images of people sitting cross-legged to meditate; that position can be uncomfortable for most people. Sit comfortably, with your spine tall, and your chin tucked down slightly. Most importantly, find the meditation position that's most comfortable for you. The ideal meditation place for most people is sitting on a chair

or couch, arms and legs uncrossed, feet flat on the floor with support underneath your backside so that your back is upright. Keep your palms open and rest them on your knees. This position helps in the free flow of life force energy.

9. **Wear comfortable clothes.**
   There are no rules for clothing in meditation, and any clothing is acceptable. Loose and comfortable clothes allow you to breathe freely and sit more comfortably. If you are meditating at work and your clothes are tight, see if you can loosen them up.

10. **Keep it short.**
    Commit to short meditation sessions and gradually increase. If you are too enthusiastic at the beginning and try to do 45-minute sessions, there's a good chance you will get discouraged and stop. It's better to meditate for short periods each day to create a consistent habit. You can start with one or two minutes and gradually increase your time to find the right amount of time for yourself.

11. **Take a few moments to wind down and clear your mind.**
    Take a few minutes to wind down and begin your meditation practice. Diving right into meditation after an intense work meeting or family situation may not be the best approach.

12. **Start with a few deep breaths to calm the body.**
    Taking three to five progressively deep breaths at the beginning of meditation aids with blood flow and relaxes the fight or flight response. When the fight or flight response is triggered, the body gets ready for danger, but when the relaxation response is activated, the body begins to feel safe and at ease. Your breathing will return to a regular rate as you start your meditation.

13. Just breathe.

The essence of meditation is simply about repeatedly bringing your awareness back to your breath. Your breath is connected to your mind and emotions. As you slow and steady your breath, your mind is led into a more peaceful, meditative state.

14. Be realistic.

Meditation is not a magic pill—it doesn't remove all the difficulties from your life. It doesn't guarantee you will be successful in everything you try. We live in the world and have to face its reality, complete with all the challenges. The resiliency you gain from meditation enables you to deal with the challenges.

15. Don't worry about progress.

Progress is like growth was when you were a child. It's so gradual and close to you that it's sometimes hard to recognize. It's impossible to predict how your meditation practice will develop. You might meditate consistently and not think nothing is happening, but that doesn't mean you aren't progressing. We are too close to our minds to see meditation progress in the beginning. But there will be moments when you notice a substantial shift in your mind.

16. Just do it – again and again.

This point bears repeating. The best meditation tip I can offer is to keep showing up and practicing. Since your mind is always with you, there are many benefits to working with the mind. If your mind is peaceful, your perception of the world will change, and you will have a much healthier, more positive view of life. When you see things more objectively, you will experience better decision-making.

17. Remember the benefits.
As I mentioned earlier in this guide, the benefits of meditation are multitude. Personally, one profound benefit for me has been cultivating peace and calmness in my mind. Meditation also gives you the courage to look at things positively, even during challenging times. It also creates resilience and mental stamina, which is vital for people dealing with the stress and hardships of life.

18. Go into your meditation practice without expectations.
Meditation is not an instant fix to all your problems. Meditation does take practice, and it takes time to reap the benefits. Try not to approach each meditation with set expectations of how you will feel after. View each meditation session as an opportunity to get to know your mind better.

19. Be kind to yourself.
Some days will be easy breezy, and some will not. Meditation is about learning how to treat yourself with kindness regardless of what you may be experiencing at any given moment. Some days will feel easier than others. Remember that it's a meditation practice, and it's not always going to be perfect.

20. Acknowledge your emotions.
Meditation brings up positive emotions and negative emotions. Meditation helps us better recognize what our emotions are. They are fleeting thoughts and feelings that come and go. It's normal to feel happy after meditating, but feeling a bit down is also normal.

21. Get comfortable with discomfort.
People who are new to meditation and even people who have been doing it for a long time often experience

agitation, restlessness, anxiety, or unease while meditating. Don't resist your emotions. Give them your attention and permission to come and go. With time, the mind learns to recognize these emotions but gets used to not getting caught up in negative thought patterns. This skill can be beneficial during meditation and in your daily life.

22. Slowly reintroduce movement after meditating.

End your meditation session gently and without any rush. Try not to open your eyes or move around hurriedly as you end your practice. Remain present in the calm you have cultivated, and take a few moments to absorb this with a feeling of gratitude. As you approach the end of your meditation, you can gently begin to move your fingers and toes. Then you can move your hands and feet and stretch your torso, arms, and legs. Meditating is all about creating a pause in your day, so try to give yourself a few minutes before jumping into any stressful task. Easing into your next activity will make it easier to bring the skills you are learning through meditation into your daily life.

23. Take your meditative mind with you.

Before you finish meditating and progress into your day, form a clear intention for what you will do next. Whatever the task or activity, aim to carry the mindfulness you obtained during your meditation into the next task and throughout your day.

24. After meditation check-in.

After each meditation practice, try to take a moment to notice how you feel mentally, emotionally, and physically. You can do this in your mind or note it in your meditation journal. Are you calmer than you were before your session? Does your mind feel more clear and at ease? The more you can establish a connection between your meditation practice and feeling better, the more invested you'll be in practicing daily.

25. Keep a meditation journal.

We become more focused on meditation and discover the best ways to fine-tune our technique through journaling. Many people who use a journal to document their sessions have found that the meditation journal allows them to stay motivated and gain insight into the best ways to continue. A journaling habit will bring insight into your world. The journal is where you can express yourself freely, documenting everything related to your practice. A significant advantage to using a meditation journal is that you can review your meditation sessions at any given time to gain insight and clarity into your meditation experience. This makes it easy to identify habitual patterns you follow and even pinpoint distractions that prevent you from achieving peace of mind.

26. Record your excuses.

If you decide not to meditate one day, note your reason(s) in a journal. Seeing your excuse written down can help you to minimize it. That excuse won't have the same power over you in the next meditation session.

27. Don't judge.

Try to resist the urge to analyze your progress regarding whether you experience massive life shifts. Instead, the next time you meditate, take a minute at the end to notice if you feel any different from when you began the meditation. Maybe you're less stressed or more aware of how you feel? You may be tempted to judge each meditation practice as "successful" or "unsuccessful" and wonder if you are "improving." Don't do that. Mediation isn't something we ever master.

It's a life-long skill we are constantly building each day.

28. Eyes open, closed, or almost closed?

Since your eyes are one of your five senses, keeping them open may keep you focused on the world outside, which hinders your journey inward. Keeping your eyes closed during meditation allows you to rest and focus attention inside yourself. Sometimes, if you start with your eyes closed, your mind may start racing right away. A technique to counter this is to use a soft gaze. Having a gentle and steady gaze relaxes the eyes, softens the face, and releases tension during practice. Looking at a still point somewhere in your meditation space can keep your mind still. Allow your eyes to gradually close in the transition from a state of activity to a state of rest.

29. Smile.

Turning up the corners of your mouth to form a gentle smile affects your mood, helps you feel relaxed and peaceful, and enhances your meditation experience.

30. How to deal with the monkey mind and thoughts.

Don't push your thoughts away. What you resist persists. The key is not to become attached to your thoughts. Instead of attaching to your thoughts, allow them to pass by. If the thought is important, it will come back to you later. By allowing your thoughts to be, you harmonize with your thoughts. You will notice them, but they won't bug you.

31. Meditation tools and apps.

While there are no special tools needed to meditate, there are some aids that people find helpful. The following is a list of some great tools to incorporate into your practice. This is not an exhaustive list, just a starting point.

Meditations on YouTube and Spotify - The Peaceland Haven website has a blog post with some great resources to find meditations.

Meditation Apps - If you haven't learned a meditation technique you love yet or don't have a meditation studio nearby, meditation apps are a quick and convenient way to get started. An app also helps you meditate easily in comfort wherever you are. Close your eyes, relax, and follow the instructions. See the Peaceland Haven blog for recommendations for great meditation apps.

Meditation Timer - A timer can help you sit through meditation, so you don't have to look at a clock. A loud meditation timer can jar your nervous system, so using soft tones is recommended. These are great if you have time constraints. For example, if you have an important meeting after your meditation, a timer is a great tool to use.

Blanket, Sweater, or Shawl - Your body temperature often drops when you get into deeper states of rest. Beginning your meditation with something warm to cover yourself can be a good idea. If you take your meditation practice outside, a light covering can protect you from the elements of nature which may distract you.

Chair, seat, or cushion(s) - Sitting upright and comfortably is important. If it's easier for you, sit in a chair or use a meditation cushion to meditate.

Meditation Music - Meditation music can help calm your nerves and take attention away from your monkey mind. Music can relax your body by stimulating the parasympathetic nervous system and calming your physiology.

Tibetan Singing Bowl - Singing bowls are meditative tools traditionally used in various religious rituals throughout Asia. Singing bowls are instruments that produce different sounds and tones. A singing bowl helps you focus and dive deeper into a meditative state. The bowls create healing frequencies that can have a relaxing and refreshing effect.

Mala Beads - Malas are a powerful and symbolic tool to enhance and deepen your meditation practice. They are most often used in a mantra meditation practice. Apart from being beautiful, using a mala during meditation can help focus your mind and breath as you move through your practice. Rolling the beads between your fingers is a physical reminder of the intention you began to practice with and prompts you to return to your breath.

Incense and Candles - You may not have realized it, but incense and candles are meditation tools. Burning incense is regarded as an offering to both religious figures, a way to clear negative energy and help induce a relaxed state of mind. Some practitioners don't recommend burning incense during meditation but beforehand as part of your room preparation ritual. Candles can be used in your meditation practice as a technique to focus your sight and attention on the flame for a certain length of time. Candles can also add a calming atmosphere to your meditation space.

32. Get meditation instruction.

Get guidance from experienced meditation instructors and trusted sources. There are helpful adjustments you can be taught to apply to your meditation technique that can make a big difference in your practice. You may feel the need to ask questions. Learning in-person or online from a certified instructor allows you to ask questions, clarify key points, and even get feedback on your practice.

33. Find a meditation partner or join a group.

Meditating with a friend as an accountability partner, you're less likely to make excuses and more likely to show up to your practice each day. You don't have to meditate simultaneously with your partner, but having someone who wants to meditate regularly can help you establish a consistent practice. Group meditation also has excellent benefits. When you sit for meditation with a group of people, the collective energy can help you have a deeper, calmer experience. You can find meditation groups online via Facebook groups or in person via local Yoga or meditation studios in your local area.

34. Get a personalized affirmation, mantra, or meditation.
I absolutely love guided meditations in my personal practice, but another favorite for me and many other meditators is using affirmations, mantras, and custom meditations. There are lots of free ones that you can find online, but sometimes it can be helpful to get a personalized affirmation, mantra, or meditation to cater to something you are working on in your life.

35. If you can't sit still, move around.
Yes, yes… I said IT. Still and silent meditation isn't for everyone! Movement can put you into a meditative state, just like sitting in stillness can. Take a walk around the block or in nature, go for a run or bike ride, or surf the waves yourself or with a friend. It sounds simple, but sometimes getting the body moving clears the head more than being still.

I hope the information in this meditation guide has been helpful in answering basic questions about meditation and how to get started.

I'm excited for you to start your journey and would love to hear how you are getting along as you get started in your practice. Feel free to send a message via the PeacelandHaven.com website to let me know how you are getting along in your meditation journey.

Sending love and light and may you find the peace, clarity and calm you seek each time you meditate.

with love,
natalie

Ahh-mazing life is revealed in the calmness of the mind and spirit.

In the sanctuary of stillness, my soul recognizes itself. As I tune in, the parts that are forgotten come into the light of the world and make manifest all that I am here on Earth to be.

PART TWO
THE JOURNAL

Meditation Journal

DATE __ / __ / 20__

TIME	LOCATION

DURATION	METHOD

MANTRA/AFFIRMATION

MEDITATION POSITION

MEDITATION INTENTION

FEELINGS & PERCEPTIONS

I AM GRATEFUL FOR

I AM WORKING TOWARDS

I AM LETTING GO OF

ADDITIONAL NOTES

M T W T F S S

Meditation Journal

TIME	LOCATION

DURATION	METHOD

MANTRA/AFFIRMATION

MEDITATION POSITION

MEDITATION INTENTION

FEELINGS & PERCEPTIONS

I AM GRATEFUL FOR	I AM WORKING TOWARDS	I AM LETTING GO OF

ADDITIONAL NOTES

M T W T F S S

Meditation Journal

DATE __ / __ / 20__

TIME	LOCATION

DURATION	METHOD

MANTRA/AFFIRMATION

MEDITATION POSITION

MEDITATION INTENTION

....
....
....
....
....
....

FEELINGS & PERCEPTIONS

....
....
....
....
....
....

I AM GRATEFUL FOR

I AM WORKING TOWARDS

I AM LETTING GO OF

ADDITIONAL NOTES

....
....
....
....

M T W T F S S

Meditation Journal

TIME	LOCATION

DURATION	METHOD

MANTRA/AFFIRMATION

MEDITATION POSITION

MEDITATION INTENTION	FEELINGS & PERCEPTIONS

I AM GRATEFUL FOR	I AM WORKING TOWARDS	I AM LETTING GO OF

ADDITIONAL NOTES

M T W T F S S

Meditation Journal

TIME	LOCATION

DURATION	METHOD

MANTRA/AFFIRMATION

MEDITATION POSITION

MEDITATION INTENTION

FEELINGS & PERCEPTIONS

I AM GRATEFUL FOR	I AM WORKING TOWARDS	I AM LETTING GO OF

ADDITIONAL NOTES

M T W T F S S

Meditation Journal

DATE __ / __ / 20__

TIME	LOCATION

DURATION	METHOD

MANTRA/AFFIRMATION

MEDITATION POSITION

MEDITATION INTENTION

FEELINGS & PERCEPTIONS

I AM GRATEFUL FOR

I AM WORKING TOWARDS

I AM LETTING GO OF

ADDITIONAL NOTES

M T W T F S S

Meditation Journal

TIME	LOCATION

DURATION	METHOD

MANTRA/AFFIRMATION

MEDITATION POSITION

MEDITATION INTENTION	FEELINGS & PERCEPTIONS

I AM GRATEFUL FOR	I AM WORKING TOWARDS	I AM LETTING GO OF

ADDITIONAL NOTES

M T W T F S S

Meditation Journal

TIME	LOCATION

DURATION	METHOD

MANTRA/AFFIRMATION

MEDITATION POSITION

MEDITATION INTENTION

FEELINGS & PERCEPTIONS

I AM GRATEFUL FOR

I AM WORKING TOWARDS

I AM LETTING GO OF

ADDITIONAL NOTES

M T W T F S S

Meditation Journal

TIME	LOCATION

DURATION	METHOD

MANTRA/AFFIRMATION

MEDITATION POSITION

MEDITATION INTENTION

FEELINGS & PERCEPTIONS

I AM GRATEFUL FOR

I AM WORKING TOWARDS

I AM LETTING GO OF

ADDITIONAL NOTES

M T W T F S S

_____
_____
_____
_____
_____
_____
_____
_____
_____
_____
_____
_____
_____
_____
_____
_____
_____
_____
_____
_____
_____
_____
_____
_____
_____
_____
_____

Meditation Journal

TIME	LOCATION

DURATION	METHOD

MANTRA/AFFIRMATION

MEDITATION POSITION

MEDITATION INTENTION

FEELINGS & PERCEPTIONS

I AM GRATEFUL FOR	I AM WORKING TOWARDS	I AM LETTING GO OF

ADDITIONAL NOTES

M T W T F S S

Meditation Journal

TIME	LOCATION

DURATION	METHOD

MANTRA/AFFIRMATION

MEDITATION POSITION

MEDITATION INTENTION

FEELINGS & PERCEPTIONS

I AM GRATEFUL FOR

I AM WORKING TOWARDS

I AM LETTING GO OF

ADDITIONAL NOTES

M T W T F S S

Meditation Journal

TIME	LOCATION

DURATION	METHOD

MANTRA/AFFIRMATION

MEDITATION POSITION

MEDITATION INTENTION

FEELINGS & PERCEPTIONS

I AM GRATEFUL FOR

I AM WORKING TOWARDS

I AM LETTING GO OF

ADDITIONAL NOTES

M T W T F S S

Meditation Journal

TIME	LOCATION

DURATION	METHOD

MANTRA/AFFIRMATION

MEDITATION POSITION

MEDITATION INTENTION

....
....
....
....
....
....

FEELINGS & PERCEPTIONS

....
....
....
....
....
....

I AM GRATEFUL FOR	I AM WORKING TOWARDS	I AM LETTING GO OF

ADDITIONAL NOTES

....
....
....
....

84

M T W T F S S

Meditation Journal

DATE __ / __ / 20__

TIME	LOCATION

DURATION	METHOD

MANTRA/AFFIRMATION

MEDITATION POSITION

MEDITATION INTENTION

FEELINGS & PERCEPTIONS

I AM GRATEFUL FOR

I AM WORKING TOWARDS

I AM LETTING GO OF

ADDITIONAL NOTES

M T W T F S S

Meditation Journal

DATE __ / __ / 20__

TIME	LOCATION

DURATION	METHOD

MANTRA/AFFIRMATION

MEDITATION POSITION

MEDITATION INTENTION	FEELINGS & PERCEPTIONS

I AM GRATEFUL FOR	I AM WORKING TOWARDS	I AM LETTING GO OF

ADDITIONAL NOTES

M T W T F S S

Meditation Journal

TIME	LOCATION

DURATION	METHOD

MANTRA/AFFIRMATION

MEDITATION POSITION

MEDITATION INTENTION

FEELINGS & PERCEPTIONS

I AM GRATEFUL FOR

I AM WORKING TOWARDS

I AM LETTING GO OF

ADDITIONAL NOTES

M T W T F S S

Meditation Journal

TIME	LOCATION

DURATION	METHOD

MANTRA/AFFIRMATION

MEDITATION POSITION

MEDITATION INTENTION

FEELINGS & PERCEPTIONS

I AM GRATEFUL FOR

I AM WORKING TOWARDS

I AM LETTING GO OF

ADDITIONAL NOTES

M T W T F S S

Meditation Journal

TIME	LOCATION

DURATION	METHOD

MANTRA/AFFIRMATION

MEDITATION POSITION

MEDITATION INTENTION	FEELINGS & PERCEPTIONS

I AM GRATEFUL FOR	I AM WORKING TOWARDS	I AM LETTING GO OF

ADDITIONAL NOTES

M T W T F S S

Meditation Journal

DATE __ / __ / 20__

TIME	LOCATION

DURATION	METHOD

MANTRA/AFFIRMATION

MEDITATION POSITION

MEDITATION INTENTION

FEELINGS & PERCEPTIONS

I AM GRATEFUL FOR

I AM WORKING TOWARDS

I AM LETTING GO OF

ADDITIONAL NOTES

MTWTFSS

_____
_____
_____
_____
_____
_____
_____
_____
_____
_____
_____
_____
_____
_____
_____
_____
_____
_____
_____
_____
_____
_____
_____
_____
_____
_____
_____

Meditation Journal

TIME	LOCATION

DURATION	METHOD

MANTRA/AFFIRMATION

MEDITATION POSITION

MEDITATION INTENTION

FEELINGS & PERCEPTIONS

I AM GRATEFUL FOR

I AM WORKING TOWARDS

I AM LETTING GO OF

ADDITIONAL NOTES

M T W T F S S

Meditation Journal

TIME	LOCATION

DURATION	METHOD

MANTRA/AFFIRMATION

MEDITATION POSITION

MEDITATION INTENTION	FEELINGS & PERCEPTIONS

I AM GRATEFUL FOR	I AM WORKING TOWARDS	I AM LETTING GO OF

ADDITIONAL NOTES

M T W T F S S

Meditation Journal

TIME	LOCATION

DURATION	METHOD

MANTRA/AFFIRMATION

MEDITATION POSITION

MEDITATION INTENTION

FEELINGS & PERCEPTIONS

I AM GRATEFUL FOR

I AM WORKING TOWARDS

I AM LETTING GO OF

ADDITIONAL NOTES

M T W T F S S

Meditation Journal

TIME	LOCATION

DURATION	METHOD

MANTRA/AFFIRMATION

MEDITATION POSITION

MEDITATION INTENTION

FEELINGS & PERCEPTIONS

I AM GRATEFUL FOR

I AM WORKING TOWARDS

I AM LETTING GO OF

ADDITIONAL NOTES

M T W T F S S

Meditation Journal

DATE __ / __ / 20__

TIME	LOCATION

DURATION	METHOD

MANTRA/AFFIRMATION

MEDITATION POSITION

MEDITATION INTENTION

FEELINGS & PERCEPTIONS

I AM GRATEFUL FOR

I AM WORKING TOWARDS

I AM LETTING GO OF

ADDITIONAL NOTES

M T W T F S S

Meditation Journal

DATE __ / __ / 20__

TIME	LOCATION

DURATION	METHOD

MANTRA/AFFIRMATION

MEDITATION POSITION

MEDITATION INTENTION	FEELINGS & PERCEPTIONS

I AM GRATEFUL FOR	I AM WORKING TOWARDS	I AM LETTING GO OF

ADDITIONAL NOTES

M T W T F S S

Meditation Journal

TIME	LOCATION

DURATION	METHOD

MANTRA/AFFIRMATION

MEDITATION POSITION

MEDITATION INTENTION

FEELINGS & PERCEPTIONS

I AM GRATEFUL FOR

I AM WORKING TOWARDS

I AM LETTING GO OF

ADDITIONAL NOTES

M T W T F S S

_____
_____
_____
_____
_____
_____
_____
_____
_____
_____
_____
_____
_____
_____
_____
_____
_____
_____
_____
_____
_____
_____
_____
_____
_____

Meditation Journal

DATE __ / __ / 20__

TIME	LOCATION

DURATION	METHOD

MANTRA/AFFIRMATION

MEDITATION POSITION

MEDITATION INTENTION	FEELINGS & PERCEPTIONS

I AM GRATEFUL FOR	I AM WORKING TOWARDS	I AM LETTING GO OF

ADDITIONAL NOTES

M T W T F S S

Meditation Journal

TIME	LOCATION

DURATION	METHOD

MANTRA/AFFIRMATION

MEDITATION POSITION

MEDITATION INTENTION	FEELINGS & PERCEPTIONS
....	....
....	....
....	....
....	....
....	....
....	....
....	....

I AM GRATEFUL FOR	I AM WORKING TOWARDS	I AM LETTING GO OF

ADDITIONAL NOTES

....
....
....
....

M T W T F S S

Meditation Journal

TIME	LOCATION

DURATION	METHOD

MANTRA/AFFIRMATION

MEDITATION POSITION

MEDITATION INTENTION	FEELINGS & PERCEPTIONS

I AM GRATEFUL FOR	I AM WORKING TOWARDS	I AM LETTING GO OF

ADDITIONAL NOTES

M T W T F S S

Meditation Journal

TIME	LOCATION

DURATION	METHOD

MANTRA/AFFIRMATION

MEDITATION POSITION

MEDITATION INTENTION

FEELINGS & PERCEPTIONS

I AM GRATEFUL FOR

I AM WORKING TOWARDS

I AM LETTING GO OF

ADDITIONAL NOTES

M T W T F S S

Meditation Journal

TIME	LOCATION

DURATION	METHOD

MANTRA/AFFIRMATION

MEDITATION POSITION

MEDITATION INTENTION

FEELINGS & PERCEPTIONS

I AM GRATEFUL FOR	I AM WORKING TOWARDS	I AM LETTING GO OF

ADDITIONAL NOTES

M T W T F S S

Meditation Journal

DATE __ / __ / 20__

TIME	LOCATION

DURATION	METHOD

MANTRA/AFFIRMATION

MEDITATION POSITION

MEDITATION INTENTION

FEELINGS & PERCEPTIONS

I AM GRATEFUL FOR	I AM WORKING TOWARDS	I AM LETTING GO OF

ADDITIONAL NOTES

M T W T F S S

Meditation Journal

DATE __ / __ / 20__

TIME	LOCATION

DURATION	METHOD

	MANTRA/AFFIRMATION

MEDITATION POSITION

MEDITATION INTENTION	FEELINGS & PERCEPTIONS

I AM GRATEFUL FOR	I AM WORKING TOWARDS	I AM LETTING GO OF

ADDITIONAL NOTES

M T W T F S S

Meditation Journal

TIME	LOCATION

DURATION	METHOD

MANTRA/AFFIRMATION

MEDITATION POSITION

MEDITATION INTENTION

FEELINGS & PERCEPTIONS

I AM GRATEFUL FOR

I AM WORKING TOWARDS

I AM LETTING GO OF

ADDITIONAL NOTES

M T W T F S S

Meditation Journal

DATE __ / __ / 20__

TIME	LOCATION

DURATION	METHOD

MANTRA/AFFIRMATION

MEDITATION POSITION

MEDITATION INTENTION

....
....
....
....
....
....

FEELINGS & PERCEPTIONS

....
....
....
....
....
....

I AM GRATEFUL FOR	I AM WORKING TOWARDS	I AM LETTING GO OF

ADDITIONAL NOTES

....
....
....
....

M T W T F S S

Meditation Journal

TIME	LOCATION

DURATION	METHOD

MANTRA/AFFIRMATION

MEDITATION POSITION

MEDITATION INTENTION

FEELINGS & PERCEPTIONS

I AM GRATEFUL FOR

I AM WORKING TOWARDS

I AM LETTING GO OF

ADDITIONAL NOTES

M T W T F S S

Meditation Journal

TIME	LOCATION

DURATION	METHOD

MANTRA/AFFIRMATION

MEDITATION POSITION

MEDITATION INTENTION

FEELINGS & PERCEPTIONS

I AM GRATEFUL FOR

I AM WORKING TOWARDS

I AM LETTING GO OF

ADDITIONAL NOTES

M T W T F S S

Meditation Journal

TIME

LOCATION

DURATION

METHOD

MANTRA/AFFIRMATION

MEDITATION POSITION

MEDITATION INTENTION

FEELINGS & PERCEPTIONS

I AM GRATEFUL FOR

I AM WORKING TOWARDS

I AM LETTING GO OF

ADDITIONAL NOTES

M T W T F S S

Meditation Journal

TIME	LOCATION

DURATION	METHOD

MANTRA/AFFIRMATION

MEDITATION POSITION

MEDITATION INTENTION

FEELINGS & PERCEPTIONS

I AM GRATEFUL FOR

I AM WORKING TOWARDS

I AM LETTING GO OF

ADDITIONAL NOTES

MTWTFSS

Meditation Journal

TIME	LOCATION

DURATION	METHOD

MANTRA/AFFIRMATION

MEDITATION POSITION

MEDITATION INTENTION

FEELINGS & PERCEPTIONS

I AM GRATEFUL FOR

I AM WORKING TOWARDS

I AM LETTING GO OF

ADDITIONAL NOTES

M T W T F S S

Meditation Journal

DATE __ / __ / 20__

TIME	LOCATION

DURATION	METHOD

MANTRA/AFFIRMATION

MEDITATION POSITION

MEDITATION INTENTION

FEELINGS & PERCEPTIONS

I AM GRATEFUL FOR

I AM WORKING TOWARDS

I AM LETTING GO OF

ADDITIONAL NOTES

M T W T F S S

Meditation Journal

DATE __ / __ / 20__

TIME	LOCATION

DURATION	METHOD

MANTRA/AFFIRMATION

MEDITATION POSITION

MEDITATION INTENTION

FEELINGS & PERCEPTIONS

I AM GRATEFUL FOR

I AM WORKING TOWARDS

I AM LETTING GO OF

ADDITIONAL NOTES

M T W T F S S

Meditation Journal

TIME	LOCATION

DURATION	METHOD

MANTRA/AFFIRMATION

MEDITATION POSITION

MEDITATION INTENTION	FEELINGS & PERCEPTIONS

I AM GRATEFUL FOR	I AM WORKING TOWARDS	I AM LETTING GO OF

ADDITIONAL NOTES

M T W T F S S

Meditation Journal

TIME	LOCATION

DURATION	METHOD

MANTRA/AFFIRMATION

MEDITATION POSITION

MEDITATION INTENTION

FEELINGS & PERCEPTIONS

I AM GRATEFUL FOR	I AM WORKING TOWARDS	I AM LETTING GO OF

ADDITIONAL NOTES

M T W T F S S

Meditation Journal

TIME	LOCATION

DURATION	METHOD

MANTRA/AFFIRMATION

MEDITATION POSITION

MEDITATION INTENTION	FEELINGS & PERCEPTIONS

I AM GRATEFUL FOR	I AM WORKING TOWARDS	I AM LETTING GO OF

ADDITIONAL NOTES

M T W T F S S

Meditation Journal

TIME	LOCATION

DURATION	METHOD

MANTRA/AFFIRMATION

MEDITATION POSITION

MEDITATION INTENTION

FEELINGS & PERCEPTIONS

I AM GRATEFUL FOR	I AM WORKING TOWARDS	I AM LETTING GO OF

ADDITIONAL NOTES

M T W T F S S

Meditation Journal

TIME	LOCATION

DURATION	METHOD

MANTRA/AFFIRMATION

MEDITATION POSITION

MEDITATION INTENTION	FEELINGS & PERCEPTIONS

I AM GRATEFUL FOR	I AM WORKING TOWARDS	I AM LETTING GO OF

ADDITIONAL NOTES

M T W T F S S

Meditation Journal

| TIME | LOCATION |

| DURATION | METHOD |

MANTRA/AFFIRMATION

MEDITATION POSITION

| MEDITATION INTENTION | FEELINGS & PERCEPTIONS |

| I AM GRATEFUL FOR | I AM WORKING TOWARDS | I AM LETTING GO OF |

ADDITIONAL NOTES

M T W T F S S

Meditation Journal

DATE __ / __ / 20__

TIME	LOCATION

DURATION	METHOD

MANTRA/AFFIRMATION

MEDITATION POSITION

MEDITATION INTENTION

FEELINGS & PERCEPTIONS

I AM GRATEFUL FOR	I AM WORKING TOWARDS	I AM LETTING GO OF

ADDITIONAL NOTES

M T W T F S S

Meditation Journal

TIME	LOCATION

DURATION	METHOD

MANTRA/AFFIRMATION

MEDITATION POSITION

MEDITATION INTENTION

FEELINGS & PERCEPTIONS

I AM GRATEFUL FOR	I AM WORKING TOWARDS	I AM LETTING GO OF

ADDITIONAL NOTES

M T W T F S S

Meditation Journal

TIME	LOCATION

DURATION	METHOD

MANTRA/AFFIRMATION

MEDITATION POSITION

MEDITATION INTENTION

FEELINGS & PERCEPTIONS

I AM GRATEFUL FOR

I AM WORKING TOWARDS

I AM LETTING GO OF

ADDITIONAL NOTES

M T W T F S S

Meditation Journal

TIME	LOCATION

DURATION	METHOD

MANTRA/AFFIRMATION

MEDITATION POSITION

MEDITATION INTENTION	FEELINGS & PERCEPTIONS

I AM GRATEFUL FOR	I AM WORKING TOWARDS	I AM LETTING GO OF

ADDITIONAL NOTES

M T W T F S S

Meditation Journal

DATE __ / __ / 20__

TIME	LOCATION

DURATION	METHOD

MANTRA/AFFIRMATION

MEDITATION POSITION

MEDITATION INTENTION

FEELINGS & PERCEPTIONS

I AM GRATEFUL FOR

I AM WORKING TOWARDS

I AM LETTING GO OF

ADDITIONAL NOTES

M T W T F S S

Meditation Journal

DATE __ / __ / 20__

TIME	LOCATION

DURATION	METHOD

MANTRA/AFFIRMATION

MEDITATION POSITION

MEDITATION INTENTION

FEELINGS & PERCEPTIONS

I AM GRATEFUL FOR

I AM WORKING TOWARDS

I AM LETTING GO OF

ADDITIONAL NOTES

M T W T F S S

Meditation Journal

| TIME | LOCATION |

| DURATION | METHOD |

MANTRA/AFFIRMATION

MEDITATION POSITION

MEDITATION INTENTION

FEELINGS & PERCEPTIONS

I AM GRATEFUL FOR

I AM WORKING TOWARDS

I AM LETTING GO OF

ADDITIONAL NOTES

M T W T F S S

Meditation Journal

DATE __ / __ / 20__

TIME	LOCATION

DURATION	METHOD

MANTRA/AFFIRMATION

MEDITATION POSITION

MEDITATION INTENTION	FEELINGS & PERCEPTIONS

I AM GRATEFUL FOR	I AM WORKING TOWARDS	I AM LETTING GO OF

ADDITIONAL NOTES

M T W T F S S

Meditation Journal

TIME	LOCATION

DURATION	METHOD

MANTRA/AFFIRMATION

MEDITATION POSITION

MEDITATION INTENTION

FEELINGS & PERCEPTIONS

I AM GRATEFUL FOR

I AM WORKING TOWARDS

I AM LETTING GO OF

ADDITIONAL NOTES

M T W T F S S

Meditation Journal

TIME	LOCATION

DURATION	METHOD

MANTRA/AFFIRMATION

MEDITATION POSITION

MEDITATION INTENTION

FEELINGS & PERCEPTIONS

I AM GRATEFUL FOR	I AM WORKING TOWARDS	I AM LETTING GO OF

ADDITIONAL NOTES

M T W T F S S

Meditation Journal

DATE __ / __ / 20__

TIME	LOCATION

DURATION	METHOD

MANTRA/AFFIRMATION

MEDITATION POSITION

MEDITATION INTENTION

....
....
....
....
....
....

FEELINGS & PERCEPTIONS

....
....
....
....
....
....

I AM GRATEFUL FOR	I AM WORKING TOWARDS	I AM LETTING GO OF

ADDITIONAL NOTES

....
....
....
....

M T W T F S S

Meditation Journal

TIME	LOCATION

DURATION	METHOD

MANTRA/AFFIRMATION

MEDITATION POSITION

MEDITATION INTENTION

FEELINGS & PERCEPTIONS

I AM GRATEFUL FOR	I AM WORKING TOWARDS	I AM LETTING GO OF

ADDITIONAL NOTES

M T W T F S S

Meditation Journal

TIME	LOCATION

DURATION	METHOD

MANTRA/AFFIRMATION

MEDITATION POSITION

MEDITATION INTENTION

FEELINGS & PERCEPTIONS

I AM GRATEFUL FOR	I AM WORKING TOWARDS	I AM LETTING GO OF

ADDITIONAL NOTES

M T W T F S S

Meditation Journal

TIME	LOCATION

DURATION	METHOD

MANTRA/AFFIRMATION

MEDITATION POSITION

MEDITATION INTENTION

FEELINGS & PERCEPTIONS

I AM GRATEFUL FOR

I AM WORKING TOWARDS

I AM LETTING GO OF

ADDITIONAL NOTES

M T W T F S S

_____

Meditation Journal

TIME	LOCATION

DURATION	METHOD

MANTRA/AFFIRMATION

MEDITATION POSITION

MEDITATION INTENTION

FEELINGS & PERCEPTIONS

I AM GRATEFUL FOR

I AM WORKING TOWARDS

I AM LETTING GO OF

ADDITIONAL NOTES

MTWTFSS

Meditation Journal

TIME	LOCATION

DURATION	METHOD

MANTRA/AFFIRMATION

MEDITATION POSITION

MEDITATION INTENTION

FEELINGS & PERCEPTIONS

I AM GRATEFUL FOR

I AM WORKING TOWARDS

I AM LETTING GO OF

ADDITIONAL NOTES

MTWTFSS

Meditation Journal

DATE __ / __ / 20__

TIME	LOCATION

DURATION	METHOD

MANTRA/AFFIRMATION

MEDITATION POSITION

MEDITATION INTENTION

FEELINGS & PERCEPTIONS

I AM GRATEFUL FOR

I AM WORKING TOWARDS

I AM LETTING GO OF

ADDITIONAL NOTES

M T W T F S S

Meditation Journal

TIME	LOCATION

DURATION	METHOD

MANTRA/AFFIRMATION

MEDITATION POSITION

MEDITATION INTENTION	FEELINGS & PERCEPTIONS

I AM GRATEFUL FOR	I AM WORKING TOWARDS	I AM LETTING GO OF

ADDITIONAL NOTES

M T W T F S S

Meditation Journal

TIME	LOCATION

DURATION	METHOD

MANTRA/AFFIRMATION

MEDITATION POSITION

MEDITATION INTENTION

FEELINGS & PERCEPTIONS

I AM GRATEFUL FOR

I AM WORKING TOWARDS

I AM LETTING GO OF

ADDITIONAL NOTES

M T W T F S S

Meditation Journal

TIME	LOCATION

DURATION	METHOD

MANTRA/AFFIRMATION

MEDITATION POSITION

MEDITATION INTENTION

....
....
....
....
....
....

FEELINGS & PERCEPTIONS

....
....
....
....
....
....

I AM GRATEFUL FOR	I AM WORKING TOWARDS	I AM LETTING GO OF

ADDITIONAL NOTES

....
....
....
....

M T W T F S S

Meditation Journal

TIME	LOCATION

DURATION	METHOD

MANTRA/AFFIRMATION

MEDITATION POSITION

MEDITATION INTENTION

FEELINGS & PERCEPTIONS

I AM GRATEFUL FOR	I AM WORKING TOWARDS	I AM LETTING GO OF

ADDITIONAL NOTES

M T W T F S S

Meditation Journal

TIME	LOCATION

DURATION	METHOD

MANTRA/AFFIRMATION

MEDITATION POSITION

MEDITATION INTENTION

FEELINGS & PERCEPTIONS

I AM GRATEFUL FOR	I AM WORKING TOWARDS	I AM LETTING GO OF

ADDITIONAL NOTES

M T W T F S S

Meditation Journal

TIME	LOCATION

DURATION	METHOD

MANTRA/AFFIRMATION

MEDITATION POSITION

MEDITATION INTENTION

FEELINGS & PERCEPTIONS

I AM GRATEFUL FOR

I AM WORKING TOWARDS

I AM LETTING GO OF

ADDITIONAL NOTES

M T W T F S S

Meditation Journal

TIME	LOCATION

DURATION	METHOD

MANTRA/AFFIRMATION

MEDITATION POSITION

MEDITATION INTENTION

FEELINGS & PERCEPTIONS

I AM GRATEFUL FOR	I AM WORKING TOWARDS	I AM LETTING GO OF

ADDITIONAL NOTES

M T W T F S S

Meditation Journal

DATE __ / __ / 20__

TIME	LOCATION

DURATION	METHOD

MANTRA/AFFIRMATION

MEDITATION POSITION

MEDITATION INTENTION

FEELINGS & PERCEPTIONS

I AM GRATEFUL FOR

I AM WORKING TOWARDS

I AM LETTING GO OF

ADDITIONAL NOTES

M T W T F S S

Meditation Journal

DATE __ / __ / 20__

| TIME | LOCATION |

| DURATION | METHOD |

MANTRA/AFFIRMATION

MEDITATION POSITION

MEDITATION INTENTION

FEELINGS & PERCEPTIONS

I AM GRATEFUL FOR

I AM WORKING TOWARDS

I AM LETTING GO OF

ADDITIONAL NOTES

M T W T F S S

Meditation Journal

TIME	LOCATION

DURATION	METHOD

MANTRA/AFFIRMATION

MEDITATION POSITION

MEDITATION INTENTION	FEELINGS & PERCEPTIONS

I AM GRATEFUL FOR	I AM WORKING TOWARDS	I AM LETTING GO OF

ADDITIONAL NOTES

M T W T F S S

Meditation Journal

DATE __ / __ / 20__

TIME	LOCATION

DURATION	METHOD

MANTRA/AFFIRMATION

MEDITATION POSITION

MEDITATION INTENTION

FEELINGS & PERCEPTIONS

I AM GRATEFUL FOR

I AM WORKING TOWARDS

I AM LETTING GO OF

ADDITIONAL NOTES

M T W T F S S

Meditation Journal

DATE __ / __ / 20__

TIME	LOCATION

DURATION	METHOD

MANTRA/AFFIRMATION

MEDITATION POSITION

MEDITATION INTENTION

FEELINGS & PERCEPTIONS

I AM GRATEFUL FOR	I AM WORKING TOWARDS	I AM LETTING GO OF

ADDITIONAL NOTES

M T W T F S S

Meditation Journal

TIME	LOCATION

DURATION	METHOD

MANTRA/AFFIRMATION

MEDITATION POSITION

MEDITATION INTENTION

FEELINGS & PERCEPTIONS

I AM GRATEFUL FOR

I AM WORKING TOWARDS

I AM LETTING GO OF

ADDITIONAL NOTES

M T W T F S S

Meditation Journal

DATE __ / __ / 20__

TIME	LOCATION

DURATION	METHOD

MANTRA/AFFIRMATION

MEDITATION POSITION

MEDITATION INTENTION

FEELINGS & PERCEPTIONS

I AM GRATEFUL FOR

I AM WORKING TOWARDS

I AM LETTING GO OF

ADDITIONAL NOTES

M T W T F S S

Meditation Journal

DATE __ / __ / 20__

TIME	LOCATION

DURATION	METHOD

MANTRA/AFFIRMATION

MEDITATION POSITION

MEDITATION INTENTION	FEELINGS & PERCEPTIONS

I AM GRATEFUL FOR	I AM WORKING TOWARDS	I AM LETTING GO OF

ADDITIONAL NOTES

M T W T F S S

Meditation Journal

TIME	LOCATION

DURATION	METHOD

MANTRA/AFFIRMATION

MEDITATION POSITION

MEDITATION INTENTION

FEELINGS & PERCEPTIONS

I AM GRATEFUL FOR

I AM WORKING TOWARDS

I AM LETTING GO OF

ADDITIONAL NOTES

M T W T F S S

Meditation Journal

TIME	LOCATION

DURATION	METHOD

MANTRA/AFFIRMATION

MEDITATION POSITION

MEDITATION INTENTION

FEELINGS & PERCEPTIONS

I AM GRATEFUL FOR

I AM WORKING TOWARDS

I AM LETTING GO OF

ADDITIONAL NOTES

M T W T F S S

Meditation Journal

TIME	LOCATION

DURATION	METHOD

MANTRA/AFFIRMATION

MEDITATION POSITION

MEDITATION INTENTION

FEELINGS & PERCEPTIONS

I AM GRATEFUL FOR

I AM WORKING TOWARDS

I AM LETTING GO OF

ADDITIONAL NOTES

M T W T F S S

Meditation Journal

TIME	LOCATION

DURATION	METHOD

MANTRA/AFFIRMATION

MEDITATION POSITION

MEDITATION INTENTION	FEELINGS & PERCEPTIONS

I AM GRATEFUL FOR	I AM WORKING TOWARDS	I AM LETTING GO OF

ADDITIONAL NOTES

M T W T F S S

Meditation Journal

TIME	LOCATION

DURATION	METHOD

MANTRA/AFFIRMATION

MEDITATION POSITION

MEDITATION INTENTION

FEELINGS & PERCEPTIONS

I AM GRATEFUL FOR	I AM WORKING TOWARDS	I AM LETTING GO OF

ADDITIONAL NOTES

M T W T F S S

Meditation Journal

DATE __ / __ / 20__

TIME	LOCATION

DURATION	METHOD

MANTRA/AFFIRMATION

MEDITATION POSITION

MEDITATION INTENTION

FEELINGS & PERCEPTIONS

I AM GRATEFUL FOR

I AM WORKING TOWARDS

I AM LETTING GO OF

ADDITIONAL NOTES

M T W T F S S

Meditation Journal

TIME	LOCATION

DURATION	METHOD

MANTRA/AFFIRMATION

MEDITATION POSITION

MEDITATION INTENTION	FEELINGS & PERCEPTIONS

I AM GRATEFUL FOR	I AM WORKING TOWARDS	I AM LETTING GO OF

ADDITIONAL NOTES

M T W T F S S

Meditation Journal

TIME	LOCATION

DURATION	METHOD

MANTRA/AFFIRMATION

MEDITATION POSITION

MEDITATION INTENTION

FEELINGS & PERCEPTIONS

I AM GRATEFUL FOR	I AM WORKING TOWARDS	I AM LETTING GO OF

ADDITIONAL NOTES

M T W T F S S

Meditation Journal

DATE __ / __ / 20__

TIME	LOCATION

DURATION	METHOD

MANTRA/AFFIRMATION

MEDITATION POSITION

MEDITATION INTENTION

FEELINGS & PERCEPTIONS

I AM GRATEFUL FOR

I AM WORKING TOWARDS

I AM LETTING GO OF

ADDITIONAL NOTES

M T W T F S S

Meditation Journal

TIME	LOCATION

DURATION	METHOD

MANTRA/AFFIRMATION

MEDITATION POSITION

MEDITATION INTENTION

FEELINGS & PERCEPTIONS

I AM GRATEFUL FOR

I AM WORKING TOWARDS

I AM LETTING GO OF

ADDITIONAL NOTES

M T W T F S S

In the sanctuary of stillness, my soul recognizes itself. As I tune in, the parts that are forgotten come into the light of the world and make manifest all that I am here on Earth to be.

ADDITIONAL RESOURCES

Please visit the meditation category on the blog at Peaceland Haven for resources to find free meditations online, meditation resources, tools, and recommendations for apps and practitioners: https://www.peacelandhaven.com/category/meditation/

Please check our Author Page on Amazon or our website https://www.peacelandhaven.com to see our selection of available guides, trackers and journals.

Your Reviews Mean So Much To Me
If you found this book to be helpful in beginning your meditation practice, please consider leaving a 5 star review on Amazon and let me know the impact the practice of meditation has had on your life.

ABOUT THE AUTHOR

Natalie Brown - Meditation Guide

I'm a mindful vocalist, spiritual seeker, songwriter/storyteller, author, and meditation guide, who unceasingly seeks to find meaning in life, understand the human condition, and help others to do the same.

It is my hope that by sharing my experiences and journey to understand myself, I can help you reach into less accessed corners of yourself so we can find peace and meaningfulness together.

I spent 30 years as a vocalist and songwriter in the commercial Pop music business. I turned to meditation and other spiritual practices on and off throughout my life, but often got off track as I chased my dreams. As I went along my journey, I noticed that meditation put me in the same space as singing by lowering the stress hormone cortisol, helping me sleep better, and rewiring my brain with a host of positive emotional qualities.

Chasing an elusive dream in commercial music for 30 years took a toll and in late 2018, I suffered a complete burnout and a serious mental health crisis. I struggled with depression, an identity crisis, extreme exhaustion, anxiety, and a serious lack of motivation for nearly 36 months.

It wasn't until my inner light felt totally burned out that I realized I needed to go back to that place of calm that singing for simply the pure joy of it (and not the 'business part') often brought me. I didn't feel ready to go back to music and singing, so once again I turned to meditation to achieve the calm, peace and clarity I craved so badly.

During this time of healing from my crisis, I underwent therapy and intensely studied meditation, spirituality, psychology, personality typology, and mindfulness. I committed to experimenting deeply with these practices as well as Emotional Freedom Techniques (EFT) tapping and other modalities to aid in my healing.

The day I chose meditation was the day things started to re-align for me. I started soaking up spiritual principles, meditation practices and anything else that helped me get aligned with my true purpose: to be a guide for others in the world.

Having practiced meditation sporadically for 20 years, I decided to go deeper into my study and practice and I became a certified meditation instructor in 2021 (Complementary Therapists Accredited Association).

As I recovered from burnout and transformed my inner life radically, I felt called to guide and teach others who might be experiencing something similar to what I have experienced with identity crisis and burnout. I resolved to combine my love of meditation, spiritual practices, writing and storytelling and embarked on a mission to create tools to help others in their healing and mindfulness journeys. This led me to create Peaceland Haven www.PeacelandHaven.com in 2022.

My mission is to use the mediums of sound and writing to help you create a peaceful, balanced, focused life that is meaningful to you.

Printed in Great Britain
by Amazon

22442821R00139